OUR ENVIRONMENT

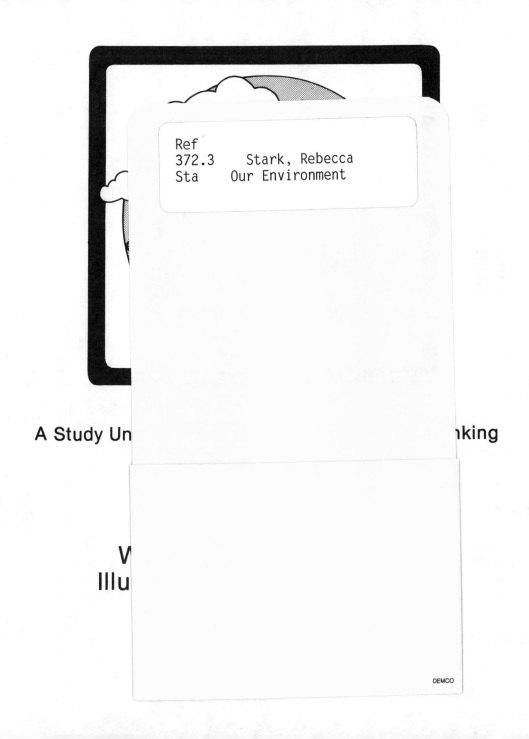

A Study Un   nking

W
Illu

DEMCO

ISBN 0-910857-89-X

© 1991 Educational Impressions, Inc., Hawthorne, NJ

EDUCATIONAL IMPRESSIONS, INC.

Hawthorne, NJ 07507

Table of Contents

INTRODUCTION

This information-based independent learning unit may be used for group, whole-class, or individual study. It is a comprehensive study unit on the environment; as such, one of its primary objectives is to introduce youngsters to basic concepts about ecology and environmental problems. Another important objective is to instill in the students an appreciation for the value of all living creatures and for Earth itself; students must learn the importance of long-term, global goals so that they, their children, and their children's children will have a safe, healthy planet on which to live. There is, however, a third and equally-important goal of the unit: the development of crucial critical and creative thinking skills. The activities were specifically designed to encourage divergent thinking, flexibility of thought, fluent production of ideas, elaboration of details, and originality. They may be adjusted to suit your particular teaching style, time limitations, and/or the ability level of the children.

Rebecca Stark

Our Environment: What Is It?

Our environment is everything that surrounds us. The air we breathe is part of our environment. The water in our streams, lakes and oceans is part of our environment. The soil in which we grow our crops is part of our environment. The earth's crust, from which we get our metals, minerals and other raw materials, is part of our environment. And we, like all other living things, are also part of the environment!

And, like other living things, we take some things from the environment and we put other things into it. Humans and other animals, for example, take oxygen from the environment. Through the process of respiration, we then put carbon dioxide into the environment. Plants, on the other hand, take carbon dioxide and water from the environment. Through a process called photosynthesis, green plants use energy from the sun to combine the carbon dioxide and water to make food. The waste product they produce is oxygen. In other words, plants put oxygen into the environment.

Every aspect of our environment is connected with another. There are many ways in which they may be connected. Living things are connected to other living things because they compete for air, water and sunshine. They are also connected to each other because of food chains. For example, a cow is connected to the grass that it eats. It is also connected to the human who drinks its milk. Usually, the changes that occur and the connections that exist maintain a balance. It is important that we care for our environment in order to preserve this balance.

There'll Be Some Changes Made

All living things interact with the environment in several basic ways: they exchange gases as they breathe; they eat plants and/or animals; and they produce body wastes. But humans interact with the environment in a way no other animal can. While other animals use what they find in the environment to fill their needs, humans *change* the environment.

Why, do you think, are humans able to change their environment in a way no other species has been able to do?

_____

_____

_____

_____

_____

Ecology

Ecology is the study of the relation of living things to their environment. It deals with the ways in which living things relate and interrelate with other living things. It also involves the ways in which living things relate to their physical surroundings. Scientists who specialize in ecology are called **ecologists.**

Earth's environment is divided into smaller environments, each with its own group of living and non-living things. We call these smaller, separate environments ecosystems. The community of life-forms that inhabit a particular ecosystem is called a biome. There are eight main types of biomes: deciduous forest, coniferous forest, tundra, grasslands, desert, tropical forest, woodland and savanna.

There are several physical conditions that make an environment suitable for some life-forms and not for others. Among the most important are:

> amount of temperature and light
> amount of rainfall and evaporation
> surface features, such as mountains and lakes
> minerals and other nutrients in the soil

For a life-form—plant or animal—to survive in a particular environment, every physical condition must meet its special needs.

Of course, living things are affected not only by their surroundings, but also by other living things! The kinds of plant life in a biome are very important in determining the kinds of animal life that can exist there. Plant-eaters can only exist if the kinds of vegetation they eat are present. Meat-eaters, in turn, depend upon the presence of the plant-eaters for their nourishment.

The specific role, or task, of an organism in an ecosystem is said to be its niche. Every species, or kind, of plant or animal must have its own niche. Sometimes it may seem as if several animals in an ecosystem have the same niche, but they don't. For example, giraffes, zebras and rhinoceroses are all grazing mammals of the African plains. But giraffes feed on trees; zebras feed on grass; and rhinos feed on brush. Each has a different niche in the same habitat.

Every biome contains a number of plant and animal communities. Each member of the community affects or is affected by another member.

What's Your Niche?

Draw at least six animals that might be found in this deciduous forest.

What is the niche of each animal in this community?

ANIMAL	NICHE

Food Chains

The dependence of living things upon other living things is most apparent in food chains. All living things need energy in order to survive. This energy gets passed along in food chains. A food chain is a kind of cycle. The energy and nutrients keep moving from non-living things to living things and back to non-living things.

Only plants have the ability to change solar energy—the energy from the sun—into the chemical energy that is stored in food. They do this through a process called photosynthesis. Green plants use the energy from the sun to turn carbon dioxide and water—the non-living things they take from the environment—into sugar. Plants are the first link in any food chain. They are called the **producers;** they produce the energy that will be passed on to the next link in the chain. However, with each step in the food chain, some of that energy is lost. It doesn't actually disappear, but it is turned into a form of energy—heat energy—that cannot be used to make food.

The next links in the food chain are all **consumers.** The first consumers are the plant-eaters. When a plant-eater eats a plant, some of the plant's energy is passed on. The nutrients, which the plant has taken from the soil, are also passed on. (Nutrients are minerals and other elements that plants and animals need in order to develop properly.) If that plant-eater should be eaten by a meat-eater, then the nutrients and some of the energy that were in the plant-eater would be passed on to the meat-eater.

A food chain may contain more than one meat-eater.

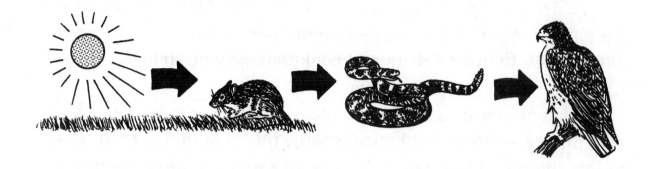

Sooner or later all living things die. When they do, they become part of a different kind of food chain. The dead organisms become food for bacteria and other **decomposers.** Bacteria also decompose waste material produced by living animals. The decomposed, or decayed, plant and animal matter is broken down. Minerals and other nutrients from the decayed matter are released into the soil. Eventually, the nutrients are dissolved by water and are taken in by living plants. And so, the cycle continues.

An Ecological Pyramid

Sometimes ecologists use pyramids to show the flow of energy in nature. At the base of an ecological pyramid is a large number* of green plants, or food producers. The next energy level is made up of a smaller number of meat-eaters. Sometimes there is a fourth or even a fifth level. The final consumers are usually, but not always, the largest. By the time the pyramid reaches the top level, most of the energy is gone.

*Note: It is actually the weight, not the number, that is important. If the base of the pyramid were an oak tree, for example, the number would be one. Thousands of insects might feed on the leaves of the one tree.

Use the field of grass as the base for an ecological pyramid. There should be at least three levels.

A Food Web

A food web is composed of interconnected food chains. Ecologists often use food webs to illustrate the many connections and inter-relationships that exist in a community.

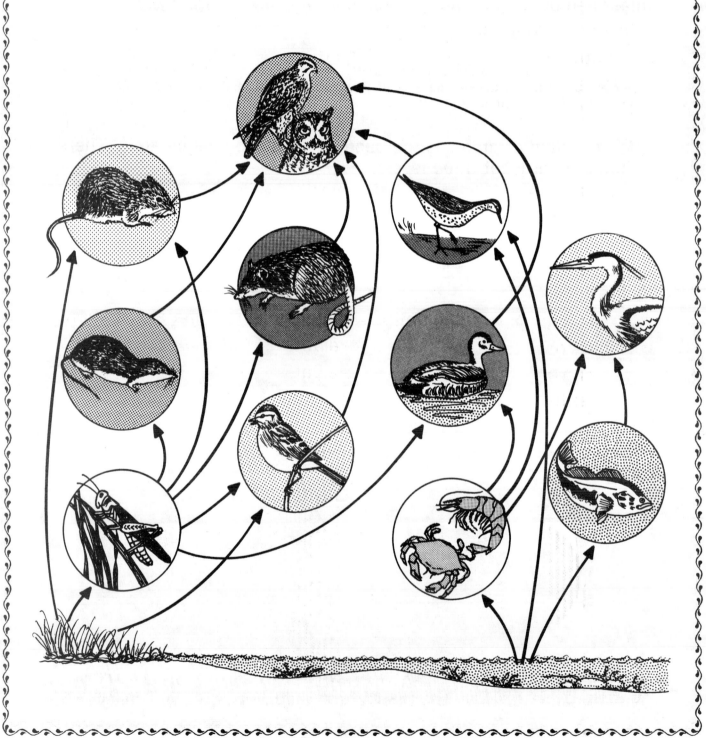

Partnerships

In addition to being links in food chains, other kinds of relationships can be found among life forms. When two different kinds of life-forms live together in close association we call it **symbiosis.** Mutualism, commensalism and parasitism are all forms of symbiotic relationships.

In **mutualism,** both life-forms benefit and neither is harmed. A lichen is an example of mutualism. It is made up of an alga and a fungus that grow together on a solid surface, such as a rock or a tree.

Commensalism is a relationship in which only one of the partners benefits. Here, too, neither is harmed. A barnacle that attaches itself to the body of a whale has a commensal relation with the whale. Only the barnacle benefits, but neither is harmed.

If one organism in a relationship benefits from the association while the other is harmed by it, the relationship is called **parasitism.** Lice living on a bird is an example of a parasitic relationship. The lice benefits; the bird is harmed.

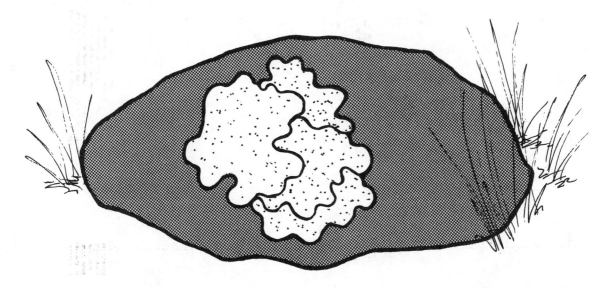

Symbiosis

Think of another symbiotic relationship. Draw a picture to illustrate that relationship. Is it an example of mutualism, commensalism or parasitism?

This is an example of: _____

Pollutants in the Air

One of the most universal of all environmental problems is air pollution. That is because air is constantly moving. The air that lingered over a factory in an industrialized city one day may hover over a wooded picnic area the next.

SMOG

Although air travels, however, smog is still a bigger problem in large cities than in rural areas. **Smog** is the hazy condition that occurs when fog is made heavier and darker by smoke and fumes. The smoke that pours out of factory chimneys contains sulfur dioxide. Cars, trucks, and other vehicles emit several other poisonous gases, including carbon monoxide, hydrocarbons, and nitrous oxides. When the amounts of these gases in the air are small, not much harm is done. Larger amounts, however, can be very harmful. In 1952 a very heavy smog in London caused over 4,000 deaths. In 1966 smog was blamed for the death of 168 people in New York City. Although laws have been passed since then to control the emissions of pollutants, smog is still a problem in many areas.

SMOKE + FOG = SMOG

The word "smog" is believed to have been invented by a physician in 1905. He was describing the poor air quality that resulted from a mixture of smoke and fog. Make up at least five new words by combining (not compounding) two existing words.

Air Pollution Affects Us All

Brainstorm all the ways in which air pollution affects life on Earth.

Acid Rain

All rain is somewhat acid. But acid rain (or snow, or hail, or fog) is rain that has been made even more acid because of pollutants in the air. Factories and power plants that burn coal and oil give off chemical compounds. So do the exhausts of automobiles and other vehicles. These compounds are mostly in the form of sulfur dioxide and nitrogen oxides. They react with water vapor in the air and form sulfuric acid and nitric acid. Because air travels, the pollution in one part of the world can affect other areas hundreds of miles away.

Acid rain affects our environment in a number of ways. Thousands of lakes, rivers, and streams have become polluted; fish and other aquatic life have died as a result. Many scientists believe that acid precipitation is harmful to trees and other plant life. They have blamed the death of thousands of acres of evergreen trees in Bavaria on acid rain. Acid rain can also affect many construction materials. Buildings, statues and other structures have been damaged by this pollution.

The best way to control acid rain is to limit the amount of chemical compounds that go into the air. There has been some success with sulfur dioxide. Devices called scrubbers can be installed in factories. They can eliminate up to 90 percent of the emissions of this compound. However, scrubbers are very expensive to install. Also, they produce a large amount of sludge, or solid waste.

Nitrogen oxides, on the other hand, have increased. While sulfur dioxide is emitted mainly from power plants and factories, nitrogen oxides are also emitted from automobiles and other vehicles. The increased use of automobiles, especially in urban areas, has caused a rise in the emission of these compounds.

A Chemistry Lesson

To understand about acid rain, you must know about acids. Here are some facts to help you:

An **element** is a substance that cannot be separated into different substances by ordinary chemical means. Carbon, hydrogen, nitrogen, chlorine, oxygen and sulfur are a few elements. Every element is represented by a symbol. The symbol for carbon is C; the one for hydrogen is H; the one for nitrogen is N; the one for chlorine is Cl; the one for oxygen is O; and the one for sulfur is S.

A **compound** is a substance that combines two or more elements. An example is carbon dioxide. It combines the elements carbon and oxygen.

An **acid** is a compound that contains the element hydrogen and, if tested, will turn litmus paper red. Many foods are mildly acidic; they have a sour taste. Oranges and lemons are acidic; they contain citric acid.

Litmus paper is a specially colored paper that indicates, or shows, whether or not a substance is acid.

Here are the names of a few acids and their formulas. Use the above information to answer the questions about these acids.

acetic acid	=	$HC_2H_3O_2$
citric acid	=	$C_6H_8O_7$
hydrochloric acid	=	HCl
nitric acid	=	HNO_3
sulfuric acid	=	H_2SO_4

1. Name the three elements found in acetic acid.

_____   _____   _____

2. Which element is found in all the acids? _____

3. Which three elements are found in nitric acid?

_____   _____   _____

4. Name the two elements in hydrochloric acid.

_____   _____

5. How many elements are in citric acid? _____

6. Which element is found in sulfuric acid and not in the other four?

_____

Where Has All The Ozone Gone?

Ozone is a form of oxygen that is created when sunlight acts upon molecules of oxygen. It forms a layer high above Earth's surface, in the part of the atmosphere called the stratosphere. There it performs a very important function. It absorbs ultraviolet radiation from the sun, acting as a protective shield for all life on Earth! Research shows that this ozone layer is being destroyed.

Scientists blame the destruction of the ozone layer on chemicals called chlorofluorocarbons, or CFC's for short. When the CFC's reach the stratosphere, they break down. Chlorine atoms are released. It is the chlorine that triggers a reaction that eventually destroys the ozone. (Studies show that there is already a hole in the ozone layer above Antarctica.)

The depletion, or lessening, of the ozone layer could have a great effect on life on Earth. An increase in ultraviolet radiation would lead to an increase in skin cancer and cataracts. It could affect the immune system. Some plant life would be damaged.

Most uses of CFC's have been banned in many nations, including the United States and Canada. For example, they are no longer used as propellants in aerosol spray cans. But there are some uses for which no suitable replacement has yet been found. To add to the problem, CFC's have a very long lifetime. Many stay in the atmosphere for as long as 300 years. Even if all future production of CFC's were eliminated, those that have already been released would continue to affect our atmosphere for at least 100 years!

It's a shame that CFC's are so harmful to the environment. They are among the most useful chemical compounds ever discovered! CFC's have been used as propellants in aerosol spray cans, as refrigerants, and as cleansing agents. They have been used in the manufacture of the plastic foam that insulates buildings; of the foam in pillows, cushions and mattresses; of the padded dashboards of automobiles; of polystyrene containers for hot foods and beverages; and of other products that we use every day. When these things are discarded and destroyed, the CFC's are released. They then rise into the stratosphere where they react upon the ozone.

What Can I Do with These?

You have just learned that the styrofoam cups you bought contain chloroflourocarbons, or CFC's. If you discard them, the CFC's will find their way into the atmosphere. What objects might you make out of the cups so that you don't have to throw them away? Try to stretch your imagination and think of some unusual ideas.

Water, Water Everywhere

Water is an important part of our environment. We drink it; we cook with it; and we bathe in it. Water helps plants grow—plants that we and other animals depend upon for food. It provides a home for the fish and seafood that we and the other animals eat.

Although there is an abundance of water on Earth, most of it is either unavailable or unusable. Only about one percent of Earth's water is suitable for human use. What's more, it is very unevenly distributed! As world population grows and industry increases, the competition for this water becomes more intense. And unfortunately, many of our human activities have side effects that pollute Earth's water—in the ground; in our lakes, rivers and streams; and in our oceans.

There are many potential sources of water pollution. Heavy metals, such as mercury and zinc; nitrogen; oil; certain bacteria and viruses; fertilizers; herbicides; toxic chemicals; radioactive materials; sediments; and decayed matter are among the variety of substances which, in excess, can lessen the quality of our water.

Groundwater

Groundwater, the water beneath the earth's surface, supplies our wells and springs. Pesticides that are banned in industrialized nations are often exported to developing nations. The toxins from the pesticides get into the groundwater. Groundwater polution is also of concern in industrialized nations. In the United States only a small portion of the groundwater is known to be polluted. But as testing becomes more common, more problems are being exposed.

"Groundwater" is a compound word. Besides "ground" and "water," what smaller words are hiding in it? You may use a letter more than once only if it is in the word "groundwater" more than once. Choose words with three or more letters.

There are more than 100 words! How many can you find?

G-R-O-U-N-D-W-A-T-E-R

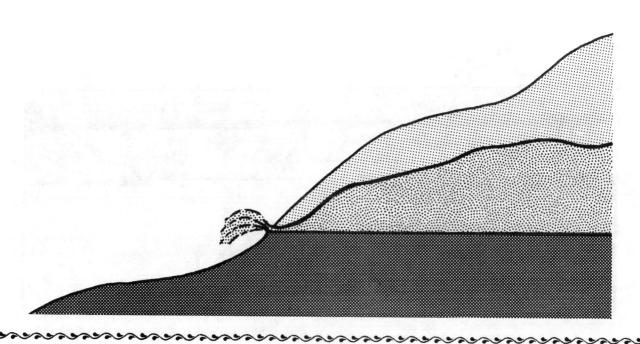

What's in the Ocean?

The ocean plays an important role in maintaining the world's environment. It provides the water necessary to maintain the water cycle. (Water moves from the atmosphere, to the earth, and back to the atmosphere.) It helps maintain the balance between the amount of oxygen and carbon dioxide in the atmosphere. It affects global climate. It provides us with food and minerals. And, of course, the ocean provides us with a source of recreation.

In spite of its evident importance, the ocean continues to be the victim of pollution. Many businesses and cities have turned to ocean dumping; they found that it was less expensive to dispose of their wastes at sea than to build landfills, advanced treatment plants or other disposal alternatives. The following are among the types of wastes that have been dumped into the ocean:

dredge spills—sand, silt, clay, rock
industrial wastes—acids, liquid wastes
medical wastes
sewage sludge—solid material that remains after sewage treatment
construction debris—cinder blocks, stones, other material
solid wastes—garbage and trash
explosives
radioactive wastes
oil

In recent years, laws have been passed to regulate the disposal of these and other wastes into our oceans.

OIL

Oil spillage is a very serious problem. In recent years, several large spills have occurred, doing great damage to beaches and to marine life. Some of the spills were caused by oil-well blowouts, tank-cleaning operations and other incidents involving drilling operations. Others were caused by accidents involving tankers that transport the oil.

One of the most publicized oil spills occurred on March 24, 1989. The tanker *Exxon Valdez* collided with a reef in Prince William Sound, Alaska. About 240,000 barrels (10.1 million gallons) of crude oil spilled into the Sound! Efforts to contain the spill were hindered by bad weather and equipment delays. A few weeks later the slick was dispersed by heavy seas. But by that time 1,100 miles (1,770 kilometers) of coastline had been polluted and thousands of animals had been killed—including some of the state's rarest species. This incident made clear the dangers of drilling in environmentally sensitive areas, such as Alaska. It also showed the need for better technology in dealing with massive spills in the open ocean.

Note: About nine months after the above incident, the Iranian tanker *Kharg 5* ruptured, spilling more than two times the amount of oil spilled by the *Exxon Valdez*. However, heavy seas broke up the oil slick within a few days and not as much damage was done.

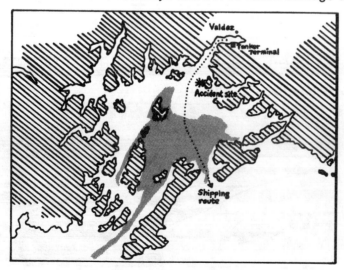

Save Our Oceans

You have been asked by an environmental group for your help. They are trying to make people aware of the need to keep our oceans and our beaches clean. Create a poster that might be placed in restaurant and shop windows in seashore areas.

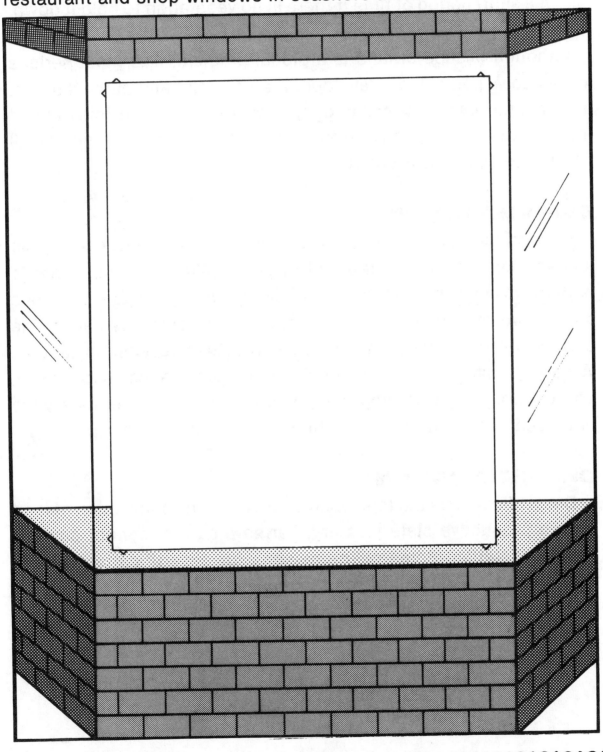

Soil Conservation

Fertile soil is one of Earth's most valuable resources. The topsoil, or upper layer of soil, is the most important. It contains the nutrients plants need for growth. Topsoil takes centuries to form, but can be lost in a short period of time if there is no vegetation to hold it down.

Although misuse of land is a global problem, it is most serious in densely populated, developing areas. Cut-and-burn farming, overgrazing, bad plowing, uncontrolled deforestation (clearing of trees), strip mining, and urbanization (the growth of cities) all contribute to the destruction of soil.

DEFORESTATION

Uncontrolled deforestation, or clearing away of trees, can lead to soil erosion. Trees hold the soil in place. Without them, there is nothing to hold the soil, and it gradually washes away. It washes away more readily in hilly areas, especially if rainfall is heavy. The problem is most severe in the tropical forests of developing nations. With each rainy season, the farmers in these areas lose a lot of soil. The erosion could be stopped if soil conservation methods were practiced: terracing crops, planting hedges, and contour plowing.

DESERTIFICATION

Desertification is the term used to describe the conversion of land from a productive state to a dry, barren area that cannot support much vegetation. Some of the reasons for desertification include soil erosion, poor drainage of irrigated lands, wasteful use of water, and overgrazing. Livestock grazing prevents the growth of plants that would hold down the soil. It is probably the number one reason for the southward expansion of the Sahara Desert.

And Then There Was Soil

Find out how soil is formed. Create a chart or diagram that could be used to teach about soil formation.

Waste Disposal

All societies must deal with the problem of waste disposal. But in industrial, urban societies the problem is greatest. It is in these areas that consumption of food, clothing, fuel and other products has reached an all-time high. Think about all the different kinds of trash you throw away every day—paper, food, metals, glass, plastic, clothing, appliances, and so on. Just disposing of this trash can be a tremendous task—especially in our more populated cities!

Years ago, most of this solid waste was placed in open dumps. They looked terrible and were a breeding ground for disease-carrying insects and other pests. Now we know that these dumps also polluted our air, our groundwater and our surface waters. Fortunately, open dumps have been banned in the United States and other nations. They have been replaced by sanitary landfills.

In a sanitary landfill, wastes are compressed so that they take up as small an area as possible. Each day the layer of waste is covered with a layer of clay or other impermeable material. "Impermeable" means that it doesn't allow fluid to pass through. These landfills are a great improvement over open dumps; however, groundwater and surface-water contamination is still possible. Another possible danger is the escape of methane gas that forms as organic wastes decompose. If care is taken not to pollute the methane gas with toxic materials, however, it can be collected and used. Probably the greatest problem of all is finding space for these landfills, especially near the cities where they're most needed. Contributing to this problem is the fact that no one wants to live near a waste disposal site. Because our consumption is not likely to decrease, waste disposal is apt to become an increasingly difficult task.

I Can't Wash Those!

Studies have shown that two to three percent of landfill space in the United States is taken up by disposable diapers. Think of all the pro's and con's for the use of disposable rather than cloth diapers. You may want to interview parents of infants and young children.

List the pro's and con's.

PRO'S   **CON'S**

Now create a conversation between two parents: one who uses disposable diapers and one who uses cloth diapers.

Parent #1:

Parent #2:

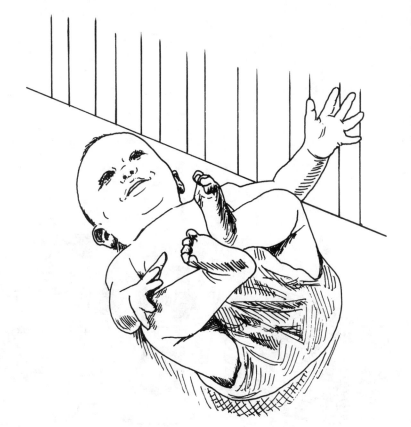

Parent #1:

Parent #2:

Parent #1:

Parent #2:

The Three R's:
Reuse, Recycle, and Reduce

One way in which we can all help lessen the problem of waste disposal is to reduce the amount of garbage we generate. This goal can be accomplished in three general ways: by buying products with the least amount of waste; by buying products that can be reused; and by recycling as many materials as possible.

Brainstorm all the ways in which you, your family, and your friends can lessen the amount of garbage you generate.

Recycling Program

By lessening the amount of waste we generate, recycling cuts down on the amount of landfill space needed. It also helps conserve energy and, therefore, helps reduce pollution and other environmental problems associated with the production of energy.

Find out as much as you can about the recycling program in your community. If there is none, research the program in a nearby town and see what you can do to get a program started in your town! Keep the following questions in mind as you do your research:

1. Is there a recycling program now in effect in your community? How long has it been in effect? If there is none, is one planned?

2. What kinds of materials are recycled? Is there a plan to add others?

3. How must the materials be divided? Are containers provided?

4. How often are recyclables collected? Are all the materials collected at the same time? Where must they be placed?

5. Does the town receive payment for the materials it collects?

Prepare a booklet that explains your town's recycling program to new residents. In the space below, write a letter to include with the booklet. It should encourage everyone to take part in the program.

Toxic Wastes

The uncontrolled disposal of hazardous chemical wastes may be the most serious environmental problem we face. These toxic substances have found their way into our air, our soil, our water and our food chains. The most publicized examples of the problems that exist involve three towns: Niagara Falls, New York; Times Beach, Missouri; and Bhopal, India. Incidents such as these make clear the need for development—and use—of safe waste-disposal methods.

LOVE CANAL

In 1976 people in the residential community of Love Canal in Niagara Falls, New York, noticed that strange things were occurring. Their trees and gardens were dying. Children's bicycle tires were disintegrating. Puddles of strange, irritating substances were appearing on the soil.

Investigators learned that the community had been built on the site of a chemical dump. For thirty years a chemical company had deposited wastes at the site. Then, in 1953, the company donated the land to the city of Niagara Falls for one dollar. Two hundred homes and an elementary school were built on it. Further study of the area showed that several toxic substances were present. Among them were dioxins and other suspected carcinogens (cancer-causing substances). Families in and around the area were evacuated and relocated, and the long, hard clean-up of the site began.

TIMES BEACH

Another potentially disastrous site was discovered in 1982 at Times Beach, near St. Louis, Missouri. Severe flooding had caused the area to be evacuated. It was then that the Center for Disease Control (CDC) discovered that the town was contaminated by toxic substances. The contamination had been created in the 1970's. Chemical wastes mixed with oil had been spread on the dirt and gravel roads in order to keep down the dust. When the CDC realized the extent of the contamination, it ordered that the town remain permanently evacuated. In February 1983 the entire town was declared unfit for human habitation and was completely buried!

BHOPAL

The most tragic incident of all occured on December 3, 1984. Toxic gas, stored in a liquid form, leaked from a pesticide plant in Bhopal, India. A cloud formed over the poor residential neighborhood that surrounded the area. The gas leak lasted less than one hour. But the chemical was so toxic that about 3,500 people were killed and thousands others were injured.

SUPERFUND

In September 1980 the United States Surgeon General Julius Richmond stated in his report to Congress that "toxic chemicals are adding to the disease burden of the United States in a significant, although not as yet precisely defined way." Later that year Congress passed a measure to create a "Superfund" to investigate and clean up toxic-waste-disposal sites.

A Rose by Any Other Name

The name Love Canal became synonomous with toxic waste contamination. In the summer of 1990 a New York state agency announced that the area was safe for resettlement. The new community would be called Black Creek Village. Some community and environmental groups want to block the resettlement. However, several people, including some former residents, have expressed an interest in buying the homes. (The homes are about 20 percent less expensive than comparable homes in nearby areas.)

Write a letter to the governor of the state. Declare either your support of the resettlement or your desire to have the decision to resettle reversed.

Fossil Fuels

Electric power, probably more than anything else, has been responsible for the high standard of living enjoyed by the industrialized nations of the world. Electricity is produced by changing some other form of energy. The mechanical energy of falling water can be converted into electrical energy. So can the heat energy of fossil fuels, such as coal, petroleum (oil) and natural gas. Demand for electricity has increased steadily during the twentieth century. It promises to keep on increasing because of our continued desire to raise our standard of living and also because of our ever-growing population!

Most of the energy consumed in the United States comes from fossil fuels. Fossil fuels are formed from the remains of plant and animal life of a previous geological time. We use these fossil fuels in many ways. Coal, oil and natural gas are all burned directly in homes and other buildings to heat them. Coal and oil are burned in power plants to produce electricity. As gasoline, petroleum moves our cars, buses and trucks. Petroleum is used to manufacture many products, such as plastic items, crayons and polyester clothing. Natural gas is used for cooking. There are environmental problems associated with the burning of all of these resources. And oil, upon which we are most dependent, is relatively scarce and exhaustible.

It is in our best interests to conserve energy in every way possible. The problems associated with fossil fuels also emphasize the need to develop and use renewable energy sources. These sources are all derived either directly or indirectly from solar energy. Renewable energy sources include direct solar energy, hydropower, geothermal energy, and wind energy. They are practically inexhaustible and they don't affect the environment like the burning of fossil fuels does.

Living Better on Less

Think of all the things that you, your friends, and your family can do to conserve energy.

Put a ✔ next to those things you are already doing.

Nuclear Energy

Concern about the effects of greenhouse gases and about the availability of fossil fuels, especially oil, has prompted some people to encourage the use of nuclear energy. Others oppose this idea. They fear that the risks involved in the production of nuclear energy are too great. These fears involve the possibility of terrorism or sabotage; the dangers of a nuclear accident; and the possibility of radioactive pollution from improper waste disposal.

GENERATING NUCLEAR POWER

A conventional power plant burns fossil fuels to generate heat to produce steam to turn a turbine to make electricity. A nuclear power plant works in a similar way. In the case of nuclear power, however, the heat is produced by the fission of the nuclear fuel, uranium, in a reactor. (Fission is the splitting of an atom.) Nuclear energy is much more powerful than chemical energy. When the nucleus of a uranium atom is split, a tremendous amount of energy is released.

RADIOACTIVITY

The main reason people fear the use of nuclear power is radioactivity. Every step in the nuclear cycle involves some degree of radiation: the mining of the uranium; the processing of the uranium; the fission of the uranium; the reprocessing of the spent nuclear fuel; and, finally, the disposal of the radioactive waste. With each step, some radiation enters the environment. Under normal operations the amounts of radiation are strictly controlled and are kept well below dangerous levels. It is the fear that an accident will occur that worries many people. While chances of such an accident are remote, the possibility does exist and it could have disastrous effects. Some people also fear that terrorists might sabotage a plant or steal nuclear materials that could be used in warfare.

All About Atoms

All matter is made up of atoms that are linked together to form molecules. Atoms are so small that they cannot be seen without the aid of a very powerful microscope. If all the atoms in a molecule are similar, it is the molecule of an element. Gold, oxygen and carbon are elements. So is uranium, which is used for nuclear fuel. If the atoms in a molecule are different, it is a molecule of a compound. Water is an example of a compound. It is made up of two different kinds of atoms—hydrogen and oxygen.

Name three other elements: _____

Name three other compounds: _____

The inner core of an atom is called its nucleus. The nucleus is made up of protons and neutrons. These protons and neutrons are packed together very tightly. The energy that is used to hold them together is the source of energy for nuclear power. Particles called electrons travel around the nucleus. What makes each kind of atom different is the number of protons, neutrons and electrons. While the number of protons and electrons of a particular element never changes, the number of neutrons sometimes does.

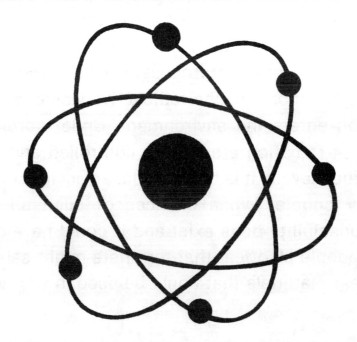

Nuclear Accidents

Many people are reluctant to use nuclear energy as an alternate to the burning of fossil fuels. The main reason for their reluctance is the fear of accidents. Although chances for such accidents are remote, the following incidents make it clear that they can occur.

THREE MILE ISLAND

On March 28, 1979, there was a malfunction at the nuclear power plant at Three Mile Island, near Harrisburg, Pennsylvania. Intense radiation was released within one of the nuclear facilities. Some radiation was also emitted into the atmosphere; however, levels were low. Luckily, the incident does not seem to have had any serious effects on the people in the area.

CHERNOBYL

Unfortunately, the people in the area around Chernobyl, about 80 miles (130 kilometers) from Kiev in the Soviet Union, were not so lucky. The nuclear accident that took place there in April 1986 was by far the most disastrous ever to occur. In fact, it was the first to directly cause fatalities. It was also the first to release a significant amount of radiation into the environment.

It is believed that there was a breakdown in the system that brings cooling water for the reactor. But human negligence—disregard for safety procedures—was the main cause of the disaster. The temperature in the reactor core rose to about 5,400°F (3,000°C). A series of explosions and fires followed, producing a massive cloud of radioactive particles. Thirty-one people died within the first few days of the incident—two from the explosions and 29 from radiation sickness. More than 200 others were treated for burns or radiation sickness. About 135,000 people had to be evacuated.

The effects of this disaster were not limited to the Soviet Union. Winds carried the radioactive clouds over much of Scandinavia and central and eastern Europe. Milk, meat and crops from these countries were contaminated. Livestock had to be destroyed. And, of course, the greatest effects may not yet be known. Millions of people were exposed to the radiation. It is feared that as many as 100,000 may develop cancer as a result of this tragic event.

Fact vs. Opinion

People make many statements regarding the use of nuclear energy. Some are based on fact and some are just opinion. Decide whether each of the following statements is fact or opinion. Write F or O in the space in front of each statement.

____ 1. Nuclear energy is produced by splitting atoms.

____ 2. Nuclear energy is dangerous.

____ 3. Nuclear energy is more powerful than chemical energy.

____ 4. Nuclear energy is safe, efficient and essential.

____ 5. Nuclear energy plants should be banned.

____ 6. We should build more nuclear energy plants.

____ 7. Uranium is radioactive.

____ 8. All matter is made up of atoms, linked together to form molecules.

____ 9. We should spend more money to make nuclear energy safe.

____ 10. France uses more nuclear energy than the United States does.

Decide whether you are for or against nuclear power. Then write a letter to the editor taking the OPPOSITE POINT OF VIEW!

Global Warming

Greenhouse effect is the term used to describe the way in which carbon dioxide and some other gases heat the atmosphere. Carbon dioxide allows the visible rays of the sun to pass through and shine upon the earth. These rays are then converted into heat energy. When the earth and the other heated surfaces on it re-radiate this heat energy, it is in the form of longer, invisible, infrared rays. Although carbon dioxide is not able to absorb the shorter, visible rays of sunlight that hit the earth, it is able to absorb these longer, invisible rays. The more carbon dioxide, the more rays that are trapped, and the hotter the atmosphere. Other gases that add to the greenhouse effect are nitrous oxide, methane and chloroflourocarbons, or CFC's.

There has been a continual build-up of these so-called greenhouse gases—especially carbon dioxide—in our atmosphere. The main cause has been the increase in the burning of fossil fuels: coal, oil and natural gas. Another reason for the build-up is the destruction of many of our forests.

Most scientists agree that the build-up of greenhouse gases will lead to a rise in world temperature, or "global warming." If the warming trend continues, it could change climate patterns in many parts of the world. Expanding seas and melted polar ice could lead to tidal flooding and beach erosion. Some island countries could become inhabitable. Fresh water supplies could become contaminated. Wind and rainfall patterns could change, allowing some parts of the world to produce more food, some less.

Although most scientists agree that there will be some rise in temperature because of the greenhouse effect, they do not agree as to how much, how fast, or with what consequence!

Where's My Island?

Imagine that it is the year 2100. Although scientists continued to warn about the dangers of global warming, not enough care was taken to cut down on the emission of greenhouse gases. Write an original story based on one or more changes that have taken place.

Spaceship Earth

Earth has been compared to a giant spaceship. Like a spaceship, there are limited amounts of resources on board. Unlike a spaceship, however, we cannot go back to the space station and refuel or re-load! Although a few of our resources on *Spaceship Earth* are renewable, most are not. And even renewable resources, such as air, water and vegetation, can be made less available through careless use.

Like a spaceship, Earth has a limited carrying capacity. There is only enough air, water, food and other resources for a limited number of people. It's easy to control the number of people who board a spaceship. It's not so easy to control the number of people who board *Spaceship Earth.*

POPULATION

The world's population has been growing at an overwhelming rate—overwhelming because Earth's resources are limited. When referring to population growth it is usual to use the term "doubling time." Doubling time is the amount of time it takes a population to double. World population doubled from 1830 to 1930, going from one to two billion people. By 1970 it almost doubled again, going to 3.6 billion people. Experts predict that it will double again by the year 2000. Will the limited resources of *Spaceship Earth* be able to support the needs of such a large population?

Too Many People

What problems might overpopulation cause? Think of the many problems—both direct and indirect—that might result.

Populations in Nature

Except for humans, populations in nature are controlled. Only a certain number of a particular animal species can occupy an area of land. How many is determined by the ability of the land to supply food, shelter, space and the other requirements of that species. The number of individual animals an environment can support without having harmful effects is called its carrying capacity.

One of the most important factors contributing to increases and decreases of animal populations is the interaction of life-forms. Suppose there were an abundance of squirrels in a particular area. The foxes that prey on them would have an abundant food supply. This, in turn, would cause the fox population to increase at a faster rate than usual. The increase in foxes would mean that more squirrels would be killed. Therefore, the squirrel population would begin to decrease. The increase in foxes and the decrease in squirrels would make it difficult for many of the foxes to find enough food. Some would starve. With less foxes to prey on the squirrels, the squirrel population would once again grow. The community would again be in balance.

Other than predation and human interference, what factors contribute to increases and decreases in populations in nature?

_____

_____

_____

_____

_____

_____

Human Affect On Other Animal Populations

Humans affect other populations in three basic ways: by over-hunting; by using pesticides; and by changing environments.

The decline of the buffalo shows what overhunting can do. Huge herds once roamed the open plains of the western part of North America. The white settlers overhunted the buffalo for many reasons. One reason was to clear the land for farming. Another was to deprive the Indians with whom they were fighting of one of their most important resources. Also, they sold the buffalo meat and hide for profit. In 1840 there were 50 million buffalo on the western plains. By 1890 there were almost none.

Human use of pesticides can affect populations other than those for which they are intended. The insecticide DDT is an example. DDT was used effectively during World War II to protect soldiers against disease-carrying lice, fleas and mosquitos. It was also used to kill the Colorado potato beetle and other insects that destroy crops. Many species of insects developed a resistance to the DDT; it did not kill them. But it did accumulate in their bodies, becoming part of the food chain. The DDT also entered the food chain by being washed away from the land by rainfall and entering the water supply. Through the food chain, eagles and other birds of prey at the end of the food chain were greatly affected. Not only did the DDT have toxic effects on them, but it also affected their eggs. It caused their shells to be very thin; many of the eggs did not survive.

The third way in which humans affect other populations is by changing the environment. If the changes we make are small, many of the living things in the environment will adapt. However, if the changes are great, most will be unable to do so.

Interference with Our Environment

All living things interact with the environment in several basic ways: they exchange gases as they breathe, they eat plants and/or animals, and they produce body wastes. But humans interfere with the environment in a way no other animal can. While other animals use what they find in their environment to fill their needs, human beings *change* the environment.

List all the things that human beings do to change the environment.

Are the human beings in your community (county, state, etc.) doing anything or planning to do anything that might affect an animal population? Draw a picture to show what they are doing.

Tell how it might affect a species living in that habitat.

_____

_____

_____

_____

_____

_____

Extinct Means Gone Forever

When a species of plant or animal life no longer exists, we say it is extinct. The dinosaurs that once roamed our planet in vast numbers are now extinct. No one is certain why the dinosaurs vanished, but they did. They are gone forever. So are the passenger pigeons. But in the case of the passenger pigeons, the reason why is clear.

In the early 1800's between five and nine *billion* passenger pigeons lived in the eastern parts of North America. There were so many of them that migrating flocks darkened the skies for days. When the settlers moved westward, however, they began to slaughter these birds by the millions. The birds were then shipped by railroad carloads and sold in city markets. Also, many of the beech and oak forests where they lived were cut down; those that were not killed by the hunters found it difficult to survive. In the second half of the century, the population declined drastically. The species officially became extinct in 1914 when the last member died in the Cincinatti Zoo.

Design a Monument

Design a monument to an extinct species.

Now create a haiku poem to engrave on a plaque to be placed on or near your monument. Haiku is a Japanese form of poetry with no rhyme. There are three lines. The first has five syllables, the second has seven and the third has five. Here is an example of a haiku poem:

Redwood Tree

Redwood, tall and strong,
A wonderful sight to see;
Are you here to stay?

_____

_____
_____
_____

Endangered Species

When a plant or animal is in danger of becoming extinct, we say that it is endangered. There are many species of endangered animals; among them are the African elephant and the blue whale. Both of these species are directly threatened by human activities.

In 1990 the Convention on International Trade in Endangered Species of Wild Fauna and Flora placed the African elephant on the list of animals dangerously close to extinction. The result was a worldwide ban on ivory trade. However, poachers continue to slaughter the African elephant for its ivory tusks.

The blue whale, the largest mammal ever to inhabit Earth, is also in danger of becoming extinct. At one time there were over 300,000 blue whales in the southern seas. Because of overhunting, it is feared that today there may only be about 200. International laws have been passed to try to save these and other endangered species of whales.

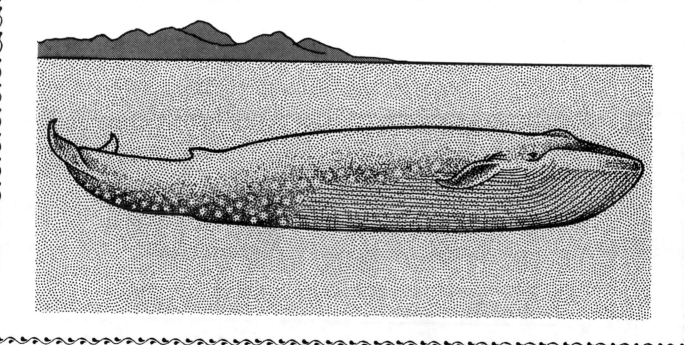

Save the . . .

Find out six other animals that are considered endangered species.

_____   _____

_____   _____

_____   _____

Create a poster to encourage people to help save an endangered species from extinction. In your poster explain the main reason the animal is in danger.

Environmentalists

An environmentalist is someone who strives to protect the natural environment. Of course, no two environmentalists share exactly the same beliefs and values. The following are some ideas shared by many environmentalists. Which do **you** agree with?

Put a ✓ in front of every idea that you believe is true.

I believe that . . .

_____ 1. All life-forms are important and their survival should be considered in our decisions.

_____ 2. All life-forms are connected in some way to other life-forms.

_____ 3. Human beings should not feel that they are more important than all other animal species.

_____ 4. We should be concerned with the quality of human life and health and should place an importance on preventive medicine, exercise and proper diet.

_____ 5. We should take a global viewpoint when it comes to matters that affect our natural environment.

_____ 6. It is important to consider how long-term results of our activities will affect future generations.

_____ 7. Waste of energy and resources should be avoided.

_____ 8. Chemicals should not be used if there is any doubt as to their safe use, storage or disposal.

_____ 9. Keeping nature "in balance" is more important than human wants.

_____ 10. We should appreciate the wilderness for its aesthetic values. (Aesthetic pertains to the sense of the beautiful.)

Just as environmentalists differ in their beliefs, so do they differ in their main concerns. For that reason, there are many different environmental groups. Which of the following concerns are important to you?

Put a ✔ in front of those problems you believe are important.

I am concerned about . . .

____ 1. Clean air and water

____ 2. Soil erosion

____ 3. Food shortages

____ 4. Allocation of fresh water to arid areas

____ 5. Availability of nonrenewable minerals

____ 6. Long-term energy supplies

____ 7. Nuclear accidents and waste disposal

____ 8. Toxic chemical wastes

____ 9. Adequate solid waste disposal sites

____ 10. Greater waste reduction through recycling

____ 11. Acid rain

____ 12. Greenhouse gases and global warming

____ 13. Depletion of the ozone layer

____ 14. Loss of natural areas due to urban sprawl

____ 15. Ocean and beach pollution

____ 16. Preservation of coral reefs

____ 17. Preservation of wilderness areas

____ 18. Protection of endangered species

____ 19. Preservation of forests, especially rain forests

____ 20. Preservation of wetlands

Other concerns:

Join Together

You have decided to form a new environmental group. Use the ideas and concerns you checked to form the basis of your policy. Add any special concerns you may have.

Summarize the policy of your new organization.

_____

_____

_____

_____

_____

_____

_____

Think of at least six names for your new group.

_____   _____

_____   _____

_____   _____

Circle the name you feel is most appropriate.

Say It on a Bumper Sticker

Think of a possible logo for your new environmental organization.
Sketch your ideas in the boxes.

Now use your best idea to design a bumper sticker.

Coral Reefs

Coral reefs occur only where waters are warm and shallow. They build up slowly from the sea floor. Coral reefs are made mostly from the stony skeletons of coral animals, from the shells of other animals, and from algae. There are different kinds of reefs. Reefs attached to land are called fringing reefs. Barrier reefs are those that are separated from the shore by a lagoon that is too deep for coral growths. An atoll is a coral island that encircles or almost encircles a lagoon. The Great Barrier Reef of Australia, at 1,250 miles (2,000 kilometres) in length, is the largest reef in the world.

Living coral animals are polyps. (Polyps are simple marine animals; they have fingerlike tentacles around the edge of their stomachs to gather food.) Corals that form reefs have stony skeletons. Cells at the base of each polyp take lime from the sea water to build up these skeletons. Most grow in colonies, with their bases connected.

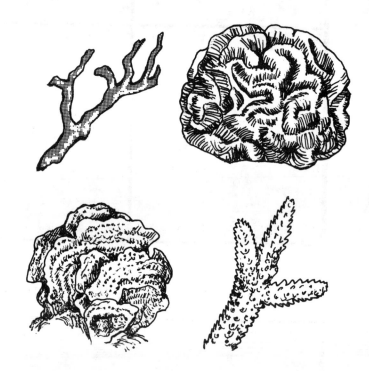

Coral reefs are rich in animal life. They provide their inhabitants with an abundance of food. However, these reefs are extremely fragile. Many of the world's reefs are being threatened by pollution. Some in the southwest Pacific are also being plagued by the spread of crown-of-thorn starfish. This species has multiplied greatly in recent years. It feeds on the soft tissues of the living coral that build the reefs.

Who Lives Here?

Unscramble these words to find out what's living in the reef!

1. **I S F H** _____

2. **A M N O E N E** _____

3. **C A L M** _____

4. **E A G L A** _____

5. **R I S H M P** _____

6. **A C R B** _____

7. **R A T S H S I F** _____

8. **E R T S Y O** _____

9. **R E T S B O L** _____

10. **L O C R A** _____

Tropical Rain Forests

Earth's tropical rain forests are disappearing at a very alarming rate. Slash-and-burn farming is the largest cause. Once a rain forest is felled, or cut down, it would take hundreds of years to regrow. Many ecologists believe that the cutting down of these rain forests will damage the balance between the amounts of oxygen and carbon dioxide in our atmosphere. It could, they say, contribute greatly to the so-called greenhouse effect. The greenhouse effect refers to the warming of Earth's surface because of the accumulation of carbon dioxide in the atmosphere.

Of course, global warming, although important, is not the only thing troubling the ecologists. Rain forests are teeming with life. Their destruction would mean a major loss of plant and animal life, including species found nowhere else. According to a report issued by the United States National Academy of Sciences, the following losses in just a 4-square-mile (10.4-square-kilometer) area were estimated:

> 750 species of trees
> 125 species of mammals
> 400 species of birds
> 100 species of reptiles
> 60 species of amphibians

And just one tree species might be home to as many as 400 insect species.

The loss of plant life from these complex ecosystems would be especially devastating. Drugs derived from plants native to rain forests have been successfully used against many diseases. Among the diseases treated by such tropical plants are malaria, Hodgkin's disease, hypertension and rheumatoid arthritis. In fact, Mr. Thomas Lovejoy of the Smithsonian Institution called the Amazon rain forest the "world's greatest pharmaceutical laboratory."

It will take worldwide cooperation to stop the destruction of these tropical forests, vital to life on Earth.

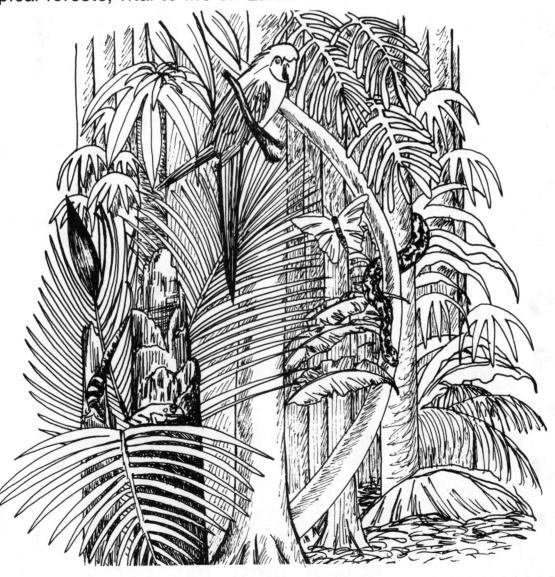

An Acrostic Poem

An acrostic poem is one in which the first letter of each line spells out a word, a name, or a message. Write an acrostic poem about the tropical rain forest.

THE RAIN FOREST

R
A
I
N
F
O
R
E
S
T

Wetlands

Wetlands, such as marshes and swamps, are lowland areas that are saturated with moisture. Many of our wetlands are being destroyed by drainage, flooding, filling-in, cultivation, and development. The Everglades is a great marsh in southern Florida. It is covered in many places with saw grass that grows to ten to fifteen feet (three to five meters) in height. The best known of its inhabitants is the alligator.

Hidden Life

In addition to the alligator, there are many other animals that inhabit the Everglades. If you read these sentences carefully, you will find the following plants and animals of the Everglades hiding in them:

cypress   heron   pines
deer   ibis   sedge (resembles grass)
egret   palm   snake

1. Miss Nak enjoys playing tennis.

2. Let her on the bus first.

3. I regret some of the things I said.

4. The crib is in the nursery.

5. Chip almost missed the train.

6. Marcy pressed her blouse with an iron.

7. "Hop in, Esther," said her mom.

8. The knife's edge was very jagged.

9. He made errors on the test.

More Critical & Creative Thinking-Skill Activities

Earth Day 2020

Earth Day 1990 (the twentieth anniversary of the first Earth Day), although primarily an American celebration, was observed in many parts of the world. There were festivals, concerts, clean-ups, fund-raisers, and television specials. Topics discussed covered everything from the need to recycle to the effect of greenhouse gases on global warming to the effort to save the rain forests. Of course, there was also celebration of Earth itself—its mountains, lakes, oceans, flowers, trees, and wildlife!

Imagine that it is Earth Day 2020. What will Earth be like? Will our air, soil, surface waters, and oceans be polluted? Will our forests be gone? Or will we have clean air; plentiful fresh, clean water; clean beaches; and forests teeming with life?

It is April 22, 2020. Describe Earth.

_____

_____

_____

_____

_____

T-Shirts for Sale

You are going to sell t-shirts at the Earth Day 2020 Fair. What do you think life on Earth will be like in 2020? Let your t-shirt reflect your ideas. Design your shirt here.

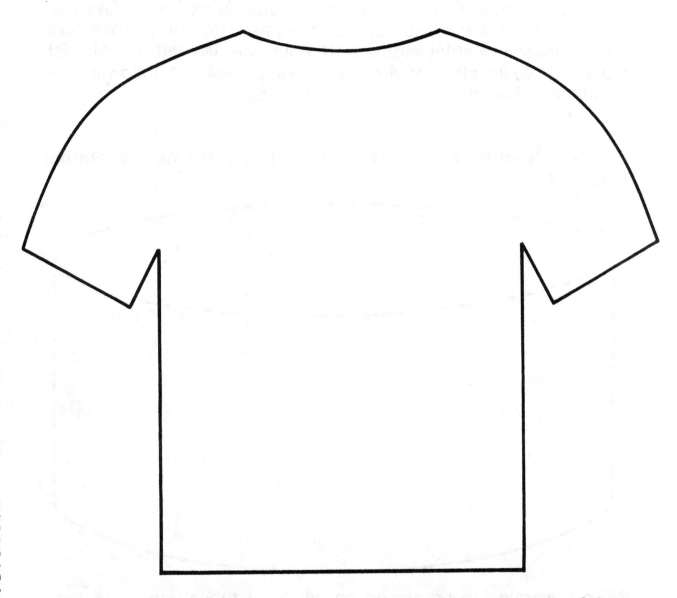

You are going to donate the money you raise from the sale of these shirts to an environmental group. The group will represent your main environmental concern in 2020. Describe its goals.

_____

_____

_____

Safe Tuna

The U.S. Congress is considering legislation that would require tuna producers to label their products. The labels would indicate whether or not the tuna was caught by methods that kill dolphins. Some companies have already begun labeling their products as "dolphin safe." The law, if passed, would assure consumers that only those companies following strict regulations would be allowed to use such labels. It would also require those companies not following the regulations to indicate that fact on the labels.

Design a label for a can of tuna caught by methods that are not harmful to dolphins.

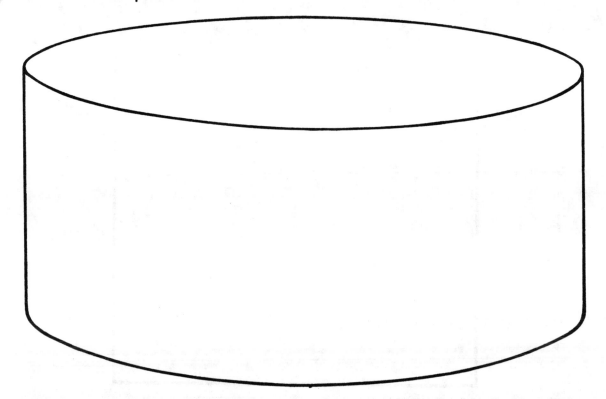

Write a warning to be placed on labels of those cans with tuna caught by methods that harm dolphins.

_____

_____

_____

_____

In Their Honor

Design a block of commemorative stamps to honor four ecologists, conservationists and/or environmentalists. They may be men or women—well-known or not so well-known—from the past, present or future.

Write a paragraph explaining why you chose those four.

_____

_____

_____

_____

_____

_____

Poster Persuasion

Which environmental problem is of most concern to you? Create a poster to encourage your friends, your neighbors, your family, your teachers, businesses and/or governments to do something to help solve this problem. Sketch your ideas on a separate sheet of paper.

Now evaluate the ideas you sketched. Which one will you choose for your poster? Follow these instructions to help you decide:

1. Write a short description of each idea.
   List the descriptions in the "Poster Ideas" column.
2. Identify 5 criteria by which to judge the ideas.
   Write them in the spaces provided.
3. Judge how each idea meets the criteria you have set.
   Use the scale to rate each idea.
4. Total the points.
   Figure out which idea best meets your criteria.
5. Decide which idea you will use for your poster.

SCALE:

5 = Excellent

4 = Good

3 = Okay

2 = Fair

1 = Poor

CRITERIA						TOTAL
POSTER IDEAS						

Best idea: _____

Reasons why: _____

_____

_____

_____

_____

_____

_____

_____

Now create a poster using the idea you chose!

You're Invited!

Plan a party with an environmental theme.

What will you serve?

_____   _____

_____   _____

_____   _____

How will you decorate?

_____

_____

_____

What kinds of activities do you plan for your guests?

_____

_____

_____

Design your invitation here.

Lesson Plan

Prepare a lesson to teach young children about an environmental problem or about a topic in ecology. Remember to keep it simple enough for the children to understand.

List at least three objectives of your lesson.

_____

_____

_____

_____

_____

List at least 5 facts that you will tell the children.

_____

_____

_____

_____

_____

_____

What questions will the class discuss?

_____

_____

_____

_____

What visual aids will you use to make your lesson interesting?

_____   _____

_____   _____

Get the Message

Think of a slogan that will make people aware of the need to SAVE OUR EARTH! For example, the slogan often used for Earth Day 1990 was "Think globally, act locally."

Use your slogan to design a button and a bookmark.

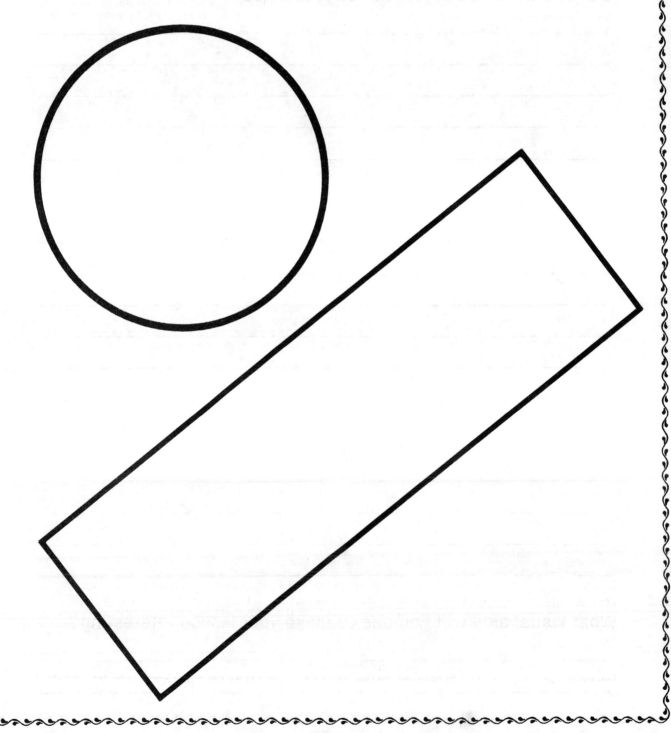

ANSWERS

Many of the activities call for original, creative answers; answers to those activities will vary greatly and are not given here.

Page 7: There'll Be Some Changes Made
The two main factors are advanced brains and thumbs. You might want to have the children tape their thumbs to the sides of their hands. Elicit from them that the use of thumbs makes many tasks easier.

Page 10: What's Your Niche?
Possible mammals include black bears, deer, bobcats, foxes, raccoons, skunks, muskrats, cottontail rabbits, squirrels, woodchucks and mice. Birds may include woodpeckers, hawks, owls, thrushes, warblers, jays and sparrows. Reptiles, amphibians and insects are also found.

Page 19: Air Pollution Affects Us All
Air pollution affects vegetation in these ways: damages leaf tissue, needles and fruit; reduces growth rate; and increases susceptibility to disease, pests and weather. It affects humans and other vertebrates in these ways: poisons them; impairs respiratory system; irritates eyes; increases susceptibility to stress-related diseases; decreases available food supply; contaminates water supply; and affects reproduction. Air pollution contributes to acid rain and the buildup of greenhouse gases. It is responsible for discoloration, erosion and decomposition of many building materials.

Page 21: A Chemistry Lesson
1. hydrogen, carbon and oxygen   2. hydrogen   3. hydrogen, nitrogen and oxygen
4. hydrogen and chloride   5. three   6. sulfur
Bring in some acidic foods such as oranges, lemons, limes and vinegar. Have the children taste them. If possible, test them with litmus paper. Test other foods that are not acidic.

Page 26: Groundwater
The 100 + words include the following: ado, age, ago, and, ant, are, around, art, ate, awe, Dane, dare, darn, dart, date, dear, dent, doe, doer, dog, donut (variation), dot, dotage, dote, down, drag, draw, drawn, drone, drown, drug, dug, ear, eat, ego, end, era, gate, gear, gnat, gnu, goad, goat, gone, got, gout, gown, grad, grade, grant, grate, grew, **ground,** grounder, grout, grow, nag, nerd, net, nod, node, not, note, oat, out, own, rag, rage, ran, rate, raw, read, red, redo, rend, rent, rot, round, rounder, rout, route, row, rower, rug, run, tad, tag, tan, tang, tear, tend, tern, toad, toe, tog, ton, tone, torn, tour, tow, tower, town, trade, tread, trend, true, turn, two, under, urge, urn, wad, wade, wag, wager, wan, wand, wander, wane, want, ward, ware, warn, wart, **water,** wear, wet, wonder, wont, wore, worn, wound and wren.

Page 27: What's in the Ocean?
You might want to advise students to cut the rings that hold together 6-packs of soda before discarding them. They often wind up in the ocean and animals sometimes get caught in them.

Page 31: And Then There Was Soil
Soil is made of tiny bits of rock and decayed plant and animal matter, or humus. It may take hundreds of years for just one inch of healthy, mature soil to develop. The first step is weathering, or the breaking up of the rock into tiny particles. Water, wind and sun are the main forces of weathering. The second step involves the action of plants. Plants that live on or near the rocks help break them up. Also, the remains of dead, decaying plants (humus) are added to the rock to make soil. The third stage involves animal action. Those animals that live in the soil mix the humus with the rock by their activity. Like plants, when animals die, their remains are added to the soil as humus.

Page 33: I Can't Wash Those
Disposable diapers take up a great deal of landfill space and are not easily biodegradable. Like other disposable items, their production wastes energy and resources. If a parent didn't wish to wash the diapers, a diaper service could be hired; the cost would be comparable to buying disposable diapers. Less landfill space would be used because there would be fewer diapers per baby. Cloth diapers could even be used as rags when no longer needed as diapers. Also, the health effects of putting dirty diapers into our landfills is not yet known. Those who favor disposable diapers refer to the time and effort saved. Some also believe the disposable diapers keep the baby drier.

Page 34: The Three R's: Reuse, Recycle and Reduce
The following are some ways to help reduce the amounts of garbage we generate: Recycle to the full extent of your community's program. Encourage your community to extend the program if necessary. Buy pro-

ducts with the least amount of excess packaging. Buy food and other products in bulk; one giant-sized box of cereal, for example, will use less packaging per ounce than a few smaller boxes. Buy food and other products that come in recyclable containers when given the choice. Refrain from buying plastic products that are not recyclable. Don't buy styrofoam products. They don't degrade easily and they also contain CFC's. Buy eggs in cardboard containers rather than styrofoam boxes. Bring your own reusable shopping bags to supermarkets and department stores. Avoid disposable items such as razors, diapers, cups, plates, dishes, and towels. Instead use items that are reusable such as cloth diapers, napkins and towels. Use rechargeable batteries. Mend clothing. Wear clothing for more than one season. Fix broken furniture and appliances. Take care of clothing and other belongings so that they last longer. Buy used goods when feasible. Make compost out of kitchen garbage.

Page 40: Living Better on Less
Most of the ideas from "The Three R's" also apply here; recycling saves energy. Also, if people waste less and reuse more, fewer goods will have to be manufactured. Other energy-saving ideas include the following: Keep homes and buildings properly insulated. Don't open and close the refrigerator unnecessarily. Turn off lights and electrical appliances when not in use. Set the thermostat higher in summer and lower in winter. Car pool. Use fuel-efficient cars. Drive within the speed limit. Ride bicycles or walk when possible. Go to the supermarket weekly rather than every one or two days. Run your other errands in a similarly efficient manner. Take energy-efficiency into account when purchasing appliances.

Page 42: All About Atoms
A few elements are silver, nitrogen, sodium, sulfur and calcium. (See the Periodic Table of the Elements for a complete list.) A few compounds are carbon dioxide, carbon monoxide, calcium carbonate and hydrogen peroxide.

Page 45: Fact vs. Opinion
1. F   2. O   3. F   4. O   5. O   6. O   7. F   8. F   9. O   10. F

Page 49: Too Many People
The following are possible consequences of overpopulation: overcrowding in certain areas; lack of fresh water due to the large demand and increased pollution problems; mineral shortages; soil erosion and desertification caused by overgrazing and overfarming; energy crisis caused by the scarcity of fossil fuels (unless alternate sources have been developed); climate changes caused by increased amounts of carbon dioxide and other greenhouse gases; famine in many parts of the world; loss of forest lands due to increased clearing of forest land for farming and lumber; loss of firewood, important as fuel in undeveloped countries; inability to properly educate and care for many of the people; loss of park and recreation areas; greater unemployment and, therefore, increased crime and poverty; scarce space for landfill and other means of waste disposal; inflation of prices due to lack of supplies; overfishing and pollution of oceans due to need to turn to the sea; increased tensions among nations due to competition for resources; and increased pollution resulting from increased chemical and pesticide use.

Page 50: Populations in Nature
These factors may contribute to increases and decreases in populations: space (animals living in overcrowded conditions seem to be affected by a type of shock disease); weather (droughts, floods, etc.); earthquakes, volcanoes and other natural disaters; disease; and competition for the same resources.

Page 53: Interference with the Environment
Humans cut down forests; drain swamps; irrigate deserts; fill in marshes and swamps; build roads and railroads; manufacture cars, ships, trucks and airplanes; burn coal, oil and gas; dig for minerals and other resources; make landfills; manufacture chemicals that find their way into the air, water and soil; build nuclear plants; litter; and so on.

Page 56: Endangered Species
Contact the Office of Endangered Species, U.S. Department of the Interior, Fish and Wildlife Service, Washington, D. C. 20240 for a current list of endangered species.

Page 63: Who Lives Here?
1. fish   2. anemone   3. clam   4. algae   5. shrimp
6. crab   7. starfish   8. oyster   9. lobster   10. coral

Page 68: Hidden Life
1. snake   2. heron   3. egret   4. ibis   5. palm
6. cypress   7. pines   8. sedge   9. deer

Page 73: In Their Honor
If the children have trouble thinking of people, you might suggest that they research the following: John Muir, Theodore Roosevelt, Rachel Carson, Gaylord Nelson, Henry David Thoreau, George Perkins Marsh, Stewart L. Udall, Aldo Leopold and/or Gifford Pinchot.